ACKNOWLEDGMENTS

I would like to thank the John Simon Guggenheim Foundation and the National Endowment for the Arts for their generous support during the writing of this book.

Grateful acknowledgment is also made to the following magazines, in which poems in this collection have previously appeared:

The American Poetry Review: "Pastoral for Derrida"
The Atlantic: "In Manufacturing," "Mule," "One of the Citizens"
The Georgia Review: "Academic Subjects," "Caught," "Every Day There Are New Memos"
The Kenyon Review: "A Blasphemy," "Dangers," "Serious Partying"
The Missouri Review: "News of the Cranes," "Winter Retreat: Homage to Martin Luther King, Jr."
Negative Capability: "Burnt Oil and Hawk"
The New Virginia Review: "On the Bearing of Waitresses"
The North American Review: "Mimosa"
Poetry: "An Explanation of the Exhibit," "Carpe Diem," "Life of Sundays"
Poetry Northwest: "Just So," "Pure Mathematics," "The Weepers"
River Styx: "My Manhood"

Transparent Gestures

Poetry by Rodney Jones

The Story They Told Us of Light (1980)
The Unborn (1985)
Transparent Gestures (1989)

Transparent Gestures

Rodney Jones

HOUGHTON MIFFLIN COMPANY · BOSTON   1989

For information about permission to reproduce selections
from this book, write to Permissions, Houghton Mifflin
Company, 2 Park Street, Boston, Massachusetts 02108.

Library of Congress Cataloging-in-Publication Data
Jones, Rodney, date.
  Transparent gestures.
  I. Title.
PS3560.05263T7   1989   811'.54   88-35783
ISBN 0-395-51062-7
ISBN 0-395-51063-5 (pbk.)

Printed in the United States of America

Book design by Robert Overholtzer

P 10 9 8 7 6 5 4 3 2 1

For Gloria

CONTENTS

I. Who Runs the Country

II. The Kitchen Gods

III. Academic Subjects

IV. The Weepers

I. Who Runs the Country

Who Runs the Country

All wig and rouge, O spry, cocksure eighty-three,
The first I met who sang the thrift of Ronnie
R. and Jesse Helms, she took me from the grounds

Where I was clipping rot from the diseased elm,
She sat me in her parlor, and then she brought me
Her prized tree. Brought it down from a high

Shelf of her camphory closet in a snowfall
Of disintegrating maps and school photographs
And set it before me on the rug. The trunk's

Olive and lime were like surplus camouflage
Or old pennies salvaged from jars. Dust muted
The leaves. But it glistened again in her talk.

It was girlhood and galloping and sources
Trembling to spell the light of 1928 or 1925.
I could hear raw jade chipped and scalloped

And bronze bubbling in the mold: the years
It took for one branch, and the three definitive
Ivory doves, like a father's patience with a son.

But the craftsmen were dead. Mao
Had killed them all. There would be only this one
Tree in Alabama, and only this one afternoon

With the old beauty. China was a thin widow
In army fatigues and America was a dowager's
Lincoln parked in a garage: heraldic, phallic —

But humming a lullaby in curves, a last cradle
Rocking from the pharmacy to the country club.
So the jade tree spoke, in a woman's voice,

Out of the enduring oil and dust, but the accent
I heard was the music that drove slaveships
And a dynastic appetite posing as a love of art.

In an instant I would take up the hated shears.
I would go back to the lawn and marble deer.
The wig would go back on the head of the manikin,

But not before I knew the riches that replace
Human beauty and saw the veins under the arms
Hardening to jade, and then the skin of nothing

When she dismissed me with one hand, she
Who had borne important children, scorned
Senators, and sat, at the end, on six boards.

One of the Citizens

What we have here is a mechanic who reads Nietzsche,
who talks of the English and the French Romantics
as he grinds the pistons; who takes apart the Christians
as he plunges the tarred sprockets and gummy bolts
into the mineral spirits that have numbed his fingers;
an existentialist who dropped out of school to enlist,
who lied and said he was eighteen, who gorged himself
all afternoon with cheese and bologna to make the weight
and guarded a Korean hill before he roofed houses,
first in East Texas, then here in North Alabama. Now
his work is logic and the sure memory of disassembly.
As he dismantles the engine, he will point out damage
and use, the bent nuts, the worn shims of uneasy agreement.
He will show you the scar behind each ear where they
put in the plates. He will tap his head like a kettle
where the shrapnel hit, and now history leaks from him,
the slow guile of diplomacy and the gold war makes,
betrayal at Yalta and the barbed wall circling Berlin.
As he sharpens the blades, he will whisper of Ruby and Ray.
As he adjusts the carburetors, he will tell you
of finer carburetors, invented in Omaha, killed by Detroit,
of deals that fall like dice in the world's casinos,
and of the commission in New York that runs everything.
Despiser of miracles, of engineers, he is as drawn
by conspiracies as his wife by the gossip of princesses,
and he longs for the definitive payola of the ultimate fix.
He will not mention the fiddle, though he played it once
in a room where farmers spun and curses were flung,
or the shelter he gouged in the clay under the kitchen.
He is the one who married early, who marshaled a crew

of cranky half-criminal boys through the incompletions,
digging ditches, setting forms for culverts and spillways
for miles along the right-of-way of the interstate;
who moved from construction to Goodyear Rubber
when the roads were finished; who quit each job because
he could not bear the bosses after he had read Kafka;
who, in his mid-forties, gave up on Sartre and Camus
and set up shop in this Quonset hut behind the welder,
repairing what comes to him, rebuilding the small engines
of lawnmowers and outboards. And what he likes best
is to break it all down, to spread it out around him
like a picnic, and to find not just what's wrong
but what's wrong and interesting — some absurd vanity,
or work, that is its own meaning — so when it's together
again and he's fired it with an easy pull of the cord,
he will almost hear himself speaking, as the steel
clicks in the single cylinder, in a language almost
like German, clean and merciless, beyond good and evil.

Winter Retreat: Homage to Martin Luther King, Jr.

There is a hotel in Baltimore where we came together,
we black and white educated and educators,
for a week of conferences, for important counsel
sanctioned by the DOE and the Carter administration,
to make certain difficult inquiries, to collate notes
on the instruction of the disabled, the deprived,
the poor, who do not score well on entrance tests,
who, failing school, must go with mop and pail
skittering across the slick floors of cafeterias,
or climb dewy girders to balance high above cities,
or, jobless, line up in the bone cold. We felt
substantive burdens lighter if we stated it right.
Very delicately, we spoke in turn. We walked
together beside the still waters of behaviorism.
Armed with graphs and charts, with new strategies
to devise objectives and determine accountability,
we empathetic black and white shone in seminar rooms.
We enunciated every word clearly and without accent.
We moved very carefully in the valley of the shadow
of the darkest agreement error. We did not digress.
We ascended the trunk of that loftiest cypress
of Latin grammar the priests could never
successfully graft onto the rough green chestnut
of the English language. We extended ourselves
with that sinuous motion of the tongue that is half
pain and almost eloquence. We black and white
politely reprioritized the parameters of our agenda
to impact equitably on the Seminole and the Eskimo.
We praised diversity and involvement, the sacrifices
of fathers and mothers. We praised the next white

Gwendolyn Brooks and the next black Robert Burns.
We deep made friends. In that hotel we glistened
over the *pommes au gratin* and the *poitrine de veau.*
The morsels of lamb flamed near where we talked.
The waiters bowed and disappeared among the ferns.
And there is a bar there, there is a large pool.
Beyond the tables of the drinkers and raconteurs,
beyond the hot tub brimming with Lebanese tourists
and the women in expensive bathing suits doing laps,
if you dive down four feet, swim out far enough,
and emerge on the other side, it is sixteen degrees.
It is sudden and very beautiful and colder
than thought, though the air frightens you at first,
not because it is cold, but because it is visible,
almost palpable, in the fog that rises from difference.
While I stood there in the cheek-numbing snow,
all Baltimore was turning blue. And what I remember
of that week of talks is nothing the record shows,
but the revelation outside, which was the city
many came to out of the fields, then the thought
that we had wanted to make the world kinder,
but, in speaking proudly, we had failed a vision.

Pussy

Not yet have I seen it published in 18-point bold.
Neither in the British nor the American anthologies.

When I say it I feel the soul of fairness and feminism
about to descend precipitately, lift me by the scruff
Of the occiput, and drop me like a clam on a rock.

I feel the preachers and Aunt Pollys of the world
Approaching with their portable altars and soap.

Long ago my mother told me write uplifting things.

But five black boys smuggled it across the bottoms
From the bootlegger's hut and slipped it in my ear —

Reuben, Clifford, Roman, Joe, and Alphonso Lemon.
I had no idea, I am very sure, what it could mean.

I thought the fishy condoms lovers had flung into ditches
Were the hog bladders my uncles had used for balls,
Scuffling and roughhousing in the lot behind the barn
Twenty-five or thirty years before I was born.

But even then I must have known it was wrong.

I was pulling a stunted bluegill from a scummy hole
In that creek everyone in my family likes to mention
Over and over because it goes by our family name,
If it goes at all, frothing the ooze of dairy farms.

Just then the five Lemons came hooting and hollering
And crowded in around me with their long poles.

I had not seen them before. I knew who they were.

Long ago my grandfather's grandfather took the ferry
Across the Tennessee River and brought back Reba,
Their grandmother's grandmother. She had been sold
To a plantation over there for four hundred dollars,
And he had to jaw two hours and feign lust for another
Lighter girl to get her back for four hundred dollars.

Everyone in my family tells this story over and over
As though we had all crossed the River Jordan and
Jehovah himself stood waiting in a white cotton robe.

That day long ago we boys lifted dozens from the hole,
Fussing though, for they kept saying it over and over.

Many times since, privately, I have spoken it in love,
But not until today have I written it down on paper,
So I remembered the fish and the history of that woman.

Even if I have told it badly, being a man. I know
The scrawniest women were worth more than the strongest men.

My Manhood

My head battered against the culvert wall, nose
letting down a dark sprig of un-Christian blood,
finally I just sat down in the ditch and gave up,
my oaths softened, all my victories compromised.
I knew the ball I had carried through cheers
would turn black and rot, what hearts I had won
would just as easily be lost. I raised my arms
and still the knee came up blunt against one ear.
The world shrieked at temple and rang in gut.
In my breath, which would not come, kings swallowed
their tongues, and in my right eye, which
would not open, Mussolini dangled from a hook.
If I could have, I would have taken it all back:
the heavy masculine god, the invincible ghost,
but I brought it on, raised it, and provoked it,
so I drank its puddle water and ate its dirt.
Finally, in the name of reason, I had to ask
the boot that kicked me to walk back to the job,
and I had to watch the bored face smugly turn
among those above me who had been my friends.
Surely defeat, like victory, is larger than man,
its legend stretched out long, imperfect as doubt.
My own ruined, at the most, two minutes,
and then work resumed, hammer and crowbar,
the boss coming, and four more forms had to
be ripped from the wall before quitting time.
What more was there to lose? The secret,
the bitter lie of triumph? The inviolable
face hidden beneath my face? I worked quietly
through the reruns where I won, and others

where I died, humiliated, slow, and small —
a wren wrapped in tissue paper, a salted slug.

This year I was never farther from all that.
This year was the breezy cafés along the Seine,
the doors of Ghiberti, the jewels of Van Eyck.
Very gently, south of Venice, the track unrolls
golden hills, tunnels, medieval villages
in the Apennines. My wife slept beside me,
a glad odor of peace, of watered leaves,
but I felt the power that blasted the gneiss
and heard the one who had laid the crossties
whisper, "On your knees, like it, now kiss it,"
and not the artisan of palaces and cathedrals
but the soldier filled me, the Hun included me,
helpless before his wrath, as he drove south,
indomitable, priapic beast who would claim
all beauty with his fists, not to love art,
but to hold it holy in his rough ideal of
dominion, in his dream of a perfect polygamy.

Dangers

From the first, I was too reluctant, achieving by dribs and drabs,
Happy to linger in shallows while others jackknifed from cliffs,
    wrong
To exact perfection from a sad piece or add notes to a proven tune;
But ever the classicist:
                      in swimming lessons, slowest to learn;
In fights, tentative, preferring the hammerlock to the jab and hook;
    cautious
In the earliest romances, choking in the clutch, fumbling the caress;
    or shy
Among the crew-cut Cupids bristling at the armory's weekend dances;
But shifty in every game, keeping it close. Always holding still
And adjuring others to go slow
                      until we leapt forward that night
    out of control
And pinned to the seats of Tyler Wilson's outlandishly unstock Ford
While, from the opposite side of the valley, scalding in each curve,
    came the black din
And brunt of Sonny Walker's highjacker Chevrolet, everyone screaming
And bearing down to be first across the bridge at Hurricane Creek.

Many trophies show us frozen: a leg poised for the hurdle, an arm
    cocked for the unanswerable spike.
What I remember through the windshield's splintering lens is time,
    a mailbox
Rushing by, the letters TURRENTINE,
                      then darkness rolling inside;
Though memory, at best, retrieves maybe six percent in studio light,
So even now I think we might have turned:
                      smart with his hands,

There is a kind of savior who blusters through the South, good
        with animals and machines,
Who surely somehow would have found a gap, through an open gate
Into a marshy cornfield
                        or up a logging road into a hillside wood.
At any rate, there is just a little while, shy of any bridge, just
        as judgment
Balances its two blind alternatives and a third accelerates head-on.
I've made a careful study: things that can only be accomplished
        in deep space,
In another language, in far history, at an almost incalculable speed.
        Courage is not included, or much foolishness.
They spin the purest glass, they split the atom, they speak with God.

They make a sort of Teflon hip and attach it with metal screws,
Only the threads upbone keep stripping
                        so they have to operate
Again and again, and what she's accomplished is more of a gait,
        really,
Than a walk, so when she moves toward me, across any room,
I think too much of my own will
                        implicated in that dragging brace.
Each step is obviously trained, and the whole earned motion full
Of muscle, plastic, and bone
                        is coordinated by nerves even the
Strictest dance does not require. She has said there is no fault,
But even in such talk,
                        grace occurs as an accident someone caused.
If what I require is a thing too certain, braided from probabilities,

There is another thing
                    articulated in the scars that saved her face —
And no right now in that night we were shaken and rolled like dice,
    no right to
Say this guilt to be alive is love, or the opposite of lucky is wrong.

On the Bearing of Waitresses

Always I thought they suffered, the way they huffed
through the Benzedrine light of waffle houses,
hustling trays of omelettes, gossiping by the grill,
or pruning passes like the too prodigal buds of roses,
and I imagined each come home to a trailer court,
the yard of bricked-in violets, the younger sister
pregnant and petulant at her manicure, the mother
with her white Bible, the father sullen in his corner.
Wasn't that the code they telegraphed in smirks?
And wasn't this disgrace, to be public and obliged,
observed like germs or despots about to be debunked?
Unlikely brides, apostles in the gospel of stereotypes,
their future was out there beyond the parked trucks,
between the beer joints and the sexless church,
the images we'd learned from hayseed troubadours —
perfume, grease, and the rending of polarizing loves.
But here in the men's place, they preserved a faint
decorum of women and, when they had shuffled past us,
settled in that realm where the brain approximates
names and rounds off the figures under uniforms.
Not to be honored or despised, but to walk as spies would,
with almost alien poise in the imperium of our disregard,
to go on steadily, even on the night of the miscarriage,
to glide, quick smile, at the periphery of appetite.
And always I had seen them listening, as time brought
and sent them, hovering and pivoting as the late
orders turned strange, *blue garden, brown wave*. Spit
in the salad, wet socks wrung into soup, and this happened.
One Sunday morning in a truckstop in Bristol, Virginia,
a rouged and pancaked half-Filipino waitress

with hair dyed the color of puffed wheat and mulberries
singled me out of the crowd of would-be bikers
and drunken husbands guzzling coffee to sober up
in time to cart their disgusted wives and children
down the long street to the First Methodist Church.
Because I had a face she trusted, she had me wait
that last tatter of unlawful night that hung there
and hung there like some cast-off underthing
caught on the spikes of a cemetery's wrought-iron fence.
And what I had waited for was no charm of flesh,
not the hard seasoning of luck, or work, or desire,
but all morning, in the sericea by the filthy city lake,
I suffered her frightened lie, how she was wanted
in Washington by the CIA, in Vegas by the FBI —
while time shook us like locks that would not break.
And I did not speak, though she kept pausing to look
back across one shoulder, as though she were needed
in the trees, but waxing her slow paragraphs into
chapters, filling the air with her glamour and her shame.

II. The Kitchen Gods

The Foolishness

After his last brindled half-Guernsey had been sold off,
after the third accident in two months, when we hid
the keys and jerked the starter from the blue Dodge,
and long after the first heart attack in the hayfield,
without mentioning it to anyone, my grandfather began
collecting plastic milk jugs and storing them in his barn,
stuffing the gunnysacks, laying whiteness down the aisle
where the halters hung like dim frames of photographs
and the hens' speckled scat whirled in cotillions of dust.
Before that he'd kept an archive of superannuated tools,
severed belts, odd linkages, screws with stripped threads,
as though, given time, the swaddling crud would unwind
from the brittle gears, the transmission frozen in reverse
would bolt the tractor forward through the unturned fields.
Or these jugs would hold other than what they'd held:
honeyed things of the spirit, bleached Saharas of wheat,
water to stanch fire, or ballast to float us past the flood.
Not that he ever slowed for fear, nor did he often
pause, cankering into dream. His wisdom was classical
and practical: to drive staples cross-grain to hold
the wire, to keep cows with small heads for easy birthing.
Sisyphus of farms, he knew the husk that transcends use
and teetered in a snaggle of plows where the spiders
were tracking rust onto the seat of the cultivator
from the upward-turning teeth of the harrow. Ahead,
morning tore at the fresh webs, the ghosts of picksacks
swayed in the crooked balance of the broken scale,
and before dawn roused the engines, he would come in secret,
with more absence than he could possibly have drunk,
bringing up from the dump, like a boy's stolen melons

or the effigies of pigs, his jugs of Pet and Meadow Gold,
building altars in troughs, raising monuments in the stable
where Charlie, the elderly gelding, had fallen and was shot.
And even when my father found them and told him
and told him, and explained again, he would not stop,
but continued, more stubbornly then, filling the loft,
rattling in the crib's musical shucks, so the field mouse
turned back from the least kernel of the spindliest cob,
and when the pigeons broke from their nests in the rafters
with a bilious cooing and a gallow's laughter of wings,
he might have thought he heard the future come suddenly,
as though the gate above him would open that easily,
completing the foolishness, and he must have known
the ancient lie of form, the empty truth of containers.

Mule

Here is this horse from a bad family, hating his burden and snaffle,
    not patient
So much as resigned to his towpath around the sorghum mill,
    but pawing the grist,
Laying back his missile ears to balk, so the single spoke of his wheel
    freezes, the gears lock.
Not sad, but stubborn, his temperament is tolerance,
    though his voice,
Old door aching on a rusty hinge, blasts the martins from their gourds,
    and he would let
Nothing go behind him: the speckled hen, the green world
    his blinders magnify.
With the heel of one ecclesiastical hoof, he would stun goats or gods.

Half-ass, garrulous priest, his religion's a hybrid appetite that feasts
    on contradictions.
In him Jefferson dreamed the end of slavery and endless fields,
    but the labor goes on
In prefabricated barns, by stalled regiments of canopied tractors,
    in offices
Where the harvest is computed to the least decimal point,
    to the last brown bowl of wheat.
Not with him, the soil yields and futures swell into the radio.
His place, finally, is to be loved as a curiosity, as an art
    almost dead, like this sulfurous creek
Of molasses he brings oozing down from the bundles of cane.

Sometimes in the library I pause suddenly and think of the mule,
    desiring, perhaps, some lost sweetness,
Some fitful husk or buttercup that blooms wildly beyond the margins.

Such a peace comes over the even rows, the bound volumes
    where the unicorn
Bows his unearthly head, where the horned gods of fecundity rear
    in the pages of the sun.
All afternoon I will think of the mule's dignity, of his shrunken lot —
While the statistics slip the tattered net of my attention,
While the lullabies erect their precise nests in the footnotes.

I like to think of the silver one of my childhood and the dark red one,
    Red.
Avuncular, puritanical, he stands on hooves as blue as quarries,
And I think his is the bray I have held back all of my life,
    in churches
Where the offering passed discreetly from one laborer to the next,
    in the factories of sleep,
Plunging a greased hand into the vat of mineral spirits.
And I think I have understood nothing better than the mule's cruelty
    and petty meanness:
How, subjugated, he will honk his incomparable impudence;
    stop for no reason;
Or, pastured with inferiors, stomp a newborn calf on a whim.

This is the mule's privilege: not to be governed badly by lashes,
    nor to be turned
Easily by praise; but, sovereign of his own spirit, to take his own time,
To meditate in the hardening compost under the rotting collars.
To sleep in wet straw. To stand for nothing but himself.
In August he will stand up to his withers in the reeking pond.

In the paradise of mules,
He will stand with the old cows, contemplative, but brooding a little
    over the sores in his shoulders,
Remembering the dull shoes of the cultivator and the jet heads
    of the mowing machine.
Being impotent and beautiful, he will dream of his useless romances.

The Kitchen Gods

Carnage in the lot: blood freckled the chopping block —
The hen's death is timeless, frantic.
Its numbskull lopped, one wing still drags
The pointless circle of a broken clock,
But the vein fades in my grandmother's arm on the ax.
The old ways fade and do not come back.
The sealed aspirin does not remember the willow.
The supermarket does not remember the barnyard.
The hounds of memory come leaping and yapping.
One morning is too large to fit inside the mouth.
My grandmother's life was a long time
Toiling between Blake's root and lightning
Yahweh and the girlish Renaissance Christ
That plugged the flue in her kitchen wall.
Early her match flamed across the carcass.
Her hand, fresh from the piano, plunged
The void bowel and set the breadcrumb heart.
The stove's eye reddened. The day's great spirit rose
From pies and casseroles. That was the house —
Reroofed, retiled, modernized, and rented out,
It will not glide up and lock among the stars.
The tenants will not find the pantry fully stocked
Or the brass boat where she kept the matches dry.
I find her stone and rue our last useless
Divisive arguments over the divinity of Christ.
Only where the religion goes on without a god
And the sandwich is wolfed down without blessing,
I think of us bowing at the table there:
The grand patriarch of the family holding forth
In staunch prayer, and the potato pie I worshiped.
The sweeter the pie, the shorter the prayer.

Caught

There is in the human voice
A quavery vowel sometimes,
More animal than meaning,
More mineral than gentle,

A slight nuance by which my
Mother would recognize lies,
Detect scorn or envy, sober
Things words would not admit,

Though it's true the best liars
Must never know they lie.
They move among good-byes
Worded like congratulations

We listen for and hear until
Some misery draws us back
To what it really was they
Obviously meant not to say.

And misery often draws us
Out to meadows or trees,
That speechless life where
Everything inhuman is true.

Mother spoke for tentative
People, illiterate, unsure.
Thinking of it her way is to
Reduce all words to tones

The wind might make anytime
With a few dead leaves. Our
Own names called in the dark
Or quail rising. Sounds that

Go straight from the ear to
The heart. There all the time,
They are a surface too clear
To see. Written down, no

Matter how right, they are too
Slow and vain as those soft
Vows we spoke in childhood to
Wild things, birds or rabbits

We meant to charm. When
My mother mentioned oaks,
They could be cut down, sawn
Into boards and nailed together

As rooms, and she was mostly
Quiet, standing in the kitchen,
Her pin rolling like law
Across plains of biscuit dough

While dark ripened, wind
Died on the tongue of each leaf.
The night broke in pieces
If she cleared her throat.

Mimosa

Among many lovely and cheap, that perfume still haunts,
and a ballad wisdom I thought I had left comes back,
but I still do not know whether to trust in the mimosa,
how much to rely on the foreign shape of the leaves,
impressionist tree made nearly bearable by its flaws,
perpetual adolescence, kept, but kept reluctantly,
as much for its soft limbs as for its sugary blossoms,
those pink rotters hastening the desecration of lawns,
those floating altars in the synagogues of hummingbirds.
It stands by my door, poor shade, implausible border.
All its length relentless, it is dying at each juncture.
It is signing itself in dust as it transcends the vents
of the air conditioner and brushes against the soffit.
It is like my two neighbors, bachelors now for a week,
the needle of the new life stinging in their pierced ears,
the new growth still itching in their scruffy beards.
They sprawl on rented cots in the trashed kitchenette,
drinking all afternoon, hot with romance and sorrow,
dialing by night the numbers of audibly erotic girls.
They stink all the time now and cry and sing at once,
but I must hear them out to believe in the mimosa,
tree of my childhood that festers in a rocky corner
where the slop and the ashes are thrown over the fence.
I must give up on my teaching to believe in its body
that won't be nailed up, that smokes but will not burn;
to trust curves more than angles, heat more than cold.
And why should I? How could I trade strategy and fear
for limp pastels and the torque of an unfocusable mass?
It is the time I put my faith in beauty and in weakness —
when I waited in the airport with no one to greet me,

and when I had to explain in that inscrutable tongue
why I had come so far to nothing and to no one —
that reminds me of when I first fell through its branches,
how my rage was mush and a pure, nerveless trembling.
Tree that is most like a weed, ubiquitous as the possum,
I have watched it slide by the ax and resurrect itself
from the stump and smother then of its own proliferation.
How many years, seasons! And today that same green
fountains out of the scars and crowns the painted stobs.
I sit on the porch, not knowing if I should salt it
this time or stake it, bind the fresh shoots with twine.
In this, at least, I am Christian. I am of two minds,
like the brontosaurus, divided into praise for the higher
parts and contempt for the roots that split the foundation,
but I know that each of my lives starts from one trunk,
each of my childhoods spreading into each of my deaths,
that what bothers me blesses me, and I hold it still
when I am ready, since the quickest cut is cleanest.

Carpe Diem

Though pretty, it rarely worked, lining seduction
with worms or being always right, like some ideal
marvel of professors, when there was time for music,
which was never words so much as time. And the subject
of those songs we prayed all adolescence to become
was not love, really, but the loneliness love betrays:
summers immersed in childhood's various waters,
warm and cool springs weaving the plaid of Brushy Lake,
and letting it all go, that guilty underwater rush.
Such easy idylls as the ice cream truck interrupts
are what we have of abandon, though we would not leave.
Even while we were there, we were begging to return,
and some of the bodies springing from bumpered posts
had already grown breasts, strange hairs at the groin
like cursive signatures we had once itched to sign.
To speak of the body is to return to that very place
where the body was most alive, not to the corpse.
Those who think of bodies most haven't seen one,
not yet. While they endure the first hormonal surge,
their bodies answer even dreams with awkward thrusts
that seem to catch them in machines and hurt memory.
And they still harbor toys: stuffed animals forgetting
their names, incomplete sets, trucks with broken grilles.
Only their guarded silences seem unseasonably adult,
though each door stonewalls the moment of flesh
until the chrysalis breaks and they fall to each other.
In lachrymose spasms. In ripe seizures of abstract joy.
Still, I don't remember what hurt me most, the blue
and womanly corpse or the slim body of my first girl.
Perhaps because the corpse was family, in my mind

it seemed to surprise some shameful act of bestial love
that stuck the eyes on open. As for the girl,
since she lay in a half-dark backseat and cringed
a little out of childish modesty, I cannot swear I saw
the breasts embarking, the slow gift of the thighs,
but staggered afterwards from the car and sat a good
twenty minutes on a rock, drunk on nothing but sense
and alien fortune. I saw us married and quarrelsome
in a trailer beside the silo on her family's dairy farm,
and then, faintly, the edge of a harder embrace,
skull against cheek, ribcage against breast. The sky
wore that raincloud look of a poorly rinsed wound.
Both times attach me to a third and ring like a chord.
I grieved them both and loved steadily as I grieved,
but why do they come together now, corpse and girl?
— admonishing me, *Be quick and gentle as you change*
seat to bed, sheet to shroud, as though I were not
already all here and late maybe for the time of my life.

News of the Cranes

Just after the tanker sank I sat eight hundred fifty miles away,
    watching
The tide push a pearly rainbow that smeared and clotted the kelp.
    The beach was crowded.
What help there was leaned on pitchforks or spread blond windrows
    of hay
Near bathers who looked slightly worried, gathering their things.
Some had come all night in caravans from as far as Oklahoma
    and now
They worked importantly under the Coast Guard's whirling blades.

I thought how, given the time, I'd march too in the battalion
    against oil,
For birds that hatch as scrotums but grow the pale down of ghosts.
And this felt moral, watching the newsman hoard his bright chance.
    He pointed inland
Toward nesting grounds where cameras and trespass were forbidden,
Then lifted a gunky gob of the black undistilled broth of gears
    and let it drop
To show his props were real. Still, many need more than pictures.

Unless they've walked under those trees, the trees in stories
    are never wholly believed.
And how can they know, how could they truly know, in Michigan
    or Idaho,
The sand of reported beaches or the blood of tropical wars?
But I had been to Aransas, where the scrub oaks root from salt
    their own magnificent deformities,
Where the whooping cranes wade all winter on pink stilts
    through the government reeds.
I believe I understood how secret and fierce their consolation.

There is a moment, just as they lift themselves from the marsh,
    when
They are like old women who hover between wheelchairs and tubs.
The bones in their wings are the splintery staves of crates
    or kites
Too cheaply made to brook the violence of the first forked limb.
Or I imagined this from what I'd seen. I watched all week.
    I didn't miss a show
Until the nests were safe, and the focus of the larger story
    moved into my room
The newly bombed ghetto and wound of some darker fascination.

Burnt Oil and Hawk

I

There in the backyard, grounded by one misflight, one tacky wing
    that had lapsed into the blackened pan,
it stood at the origin of the clement circle the hound was padding
    in the grass —
that unflinching poise,
                bald talon begrudging the tentative paw,
dog's eyes assaying the hawk's fiercer, unchanging, electric eyes,
    and I thought it
stood the way Lear had stood on the cliff, in the aftermath of power,
    of its own nature
incapable of calculating wrong or admitting, by cry, it was caught.
The figure it made,
                all lungless calm, no tremor to suggest terror.
Uninterrupted sky, where it had flown reconnaissance, and now this
strange ground for tragedy, between the scrap heap and the Briggs
    & Stratton mower:
Stranger still, when I had brought the hose from behind the house
    and turned on
those gummed feathers the full jet of spray, that it did not move
    but waited out
its cleanliness, then rose over the smokehouse and did not look back.

2

But we look back
            under the asphalt parking lot to the grassy swamp,
and the animals' stories are ours: we betray with our least surprise
    the quickened brains of crocodiles.

And because our shoulders want wings, we have stood in woods at dusk
    as birds went abruptly silent.
How purely we have listened into their night
                                though we cannot recall
our instincts with words or find home by the smell of familiar lots.
Yesterday a grocery cart
                    slipped from its rack and hurtled downhill,
barely clipping my car, but I leapt up like a deer before I thought
to say to someone
                    something, a shriek or howl — O anything to wake
that claw and thunderstorm that validate the heart.
                                        We love trees,
but yesterday, more than trees, more than the new blue radio, it was
    that cart. So my anger
lit the broccoli and turnips in their sprinkled stalls and the princess
    of cash registers and the headline
MAN TRAPPED SIX DAYS UNDER DEAD THREE HUNDRED
    SEVENTY POUND WIFE!

                            3

Kings must be privileged to only a part of the commerce of the gods
    for tragedy to exist
as Sophocles wrote it,
                    out of inspiration, dissolving our pity into fear,
and the other part is fate,
                        unwillable madness, blindness, paralysis
when we turn from the stage, and the night, the palpable unfairness
    hits us like hardened smoke.
Or this, as example: our neighbor, the science teacher, who filched
    a little thing, an easy-

to-find LP, from the discount table at Wal-Mart, was apprehended,
    so, lost his job.
His wife took the kids, the house —
                                    now when he speaks of it at all
    he means to be Job,
lowering his voice, as though he could share more than he has lost,
but is not tragic,
                either because his error is too small, or because
we ourselves are diminished, as Jeffers saw us, our best parts wild
    but compromised by the civic
and still bound to weave the net, in which we glory and are caught.

This is why he loved the hermit and chose the hawk to represent God.

                                4

Mystiques of the apocalypse! Uncarved idols abiding in the rocks!
    In all his long work,
he troubled the speechless mating of the wilderness and the machine,
and there is no forgiveness
                    when the great wind- and salt-abraded
cable over the limeworks finally snaps under the ax and lashes back.
Cut down,
        the hero cannot choose to die, but suffers his immobility
    with his knowledge —
that the stalled self mirrors a salmon expiring in the birthing pool.
That, gentled like cows, we are fed back
                                to a first, pitiless world
that regards us best through the steadily murderous eyes of hawks.
I hope we have gone past
                    the tooth-haunted meat of those thoughts.

Though we lay runways for death and grease death's perfect machines,
  I wonder what that hawk knew
to stand still and shed our burnt oil and water in a net of rainbows
  and what might free us.
What possible hand might clean us, who fear mercy more than power?

III. Academic Subjects

A Blasphemy

A girl attacked me once with a number 2 Eagle pencil
for a whiny lisping impression of a radio preacher
she must have loved more than sophistication or peace,
for she took the pencil in a whitened knuckle
and drove the point with all her weight behind it
through a thick pair of jeans, jogging it at the end
and twisting it, so the lead broke off under the skin,
an act undertaken so suddenly and dramatically
it was as though I had awakened in a strange hotel
with sirens going off and half-dressed women rushing
in every direction with kids tucked under their arms;
as though the Moslems had retaken Jerusalem for
the twelfth time, the crusaders were riding south,
and the Jews in Cadiz and Granada were packing
their bags, mapping the snowy ghettos of the north.
But where we were, it was still Tuscaloosa, late
summer, and the heat in her sparsely decorated room
we had come to together after work was so miserable
and intense the wallpaper was crimping at each seam,
the posters of daisies and horses she had pasted up
were fallen all over the floor. Whatever I thought
would happen was not going to happen. Nothing
was going to happen with any of the three billion women
of the world forever. The time it would take
for the first kindness was the wait for a Campbellite
to accept Darwin and Galileo or for all Arkansas
to embrace a black Messiah. The time it would take
for even a hand to shyly, unambiguously brush my own
was the years Bertrand Russell waited for humanism,
disarmament, and neutrality. And then she was

there, her cloth daubing at the darkly jellying wound.
In contrition, she bowed with tweezers to pick the grit.
With alcohol, she cleansed the rubbery petals.
She unspooled the white gauze and spread the balm of mercy.
Because she loved Christ, she forgave me. And what
was that all about? I wondered, walking home
through the familiar streets, the steeple of each church
raised like a beneficent weapon, the mark of the heretic
on my thigh, and mockery was still the unforgivable sin.

Academic Subjects

In the middle of the fourteenth century, I fell asleep,
    profoundly,
Between the time the Turks marched upward into Armenia
    and the time the plague leveled Sardinia.
I fell beyond amphetamines, beyond caffeine and nicotine,
    this side of the border of Arcadia.
A kind of glandular hurricane blew me down corridors
    of flesh
And through the torrid picture windows of Copenhagen.
    While I floated
The whirring of sewing machines turned into violins,
And the harvester, reaching up into dark branches,
    gathered,
Instead of oranges, the sullen breasts of his Dolores.

In the middle of the page, where the battered moth hid
    the fructifying verb, I lost my place.
The notes were no less bright — nor the alchemizing dates
    limned in yellow and lavender.
But the facts were stormclouds drifting. The last facts,
    as they dissolved,
Were like root-hollowed banks plunging into muddy rivers.
And I was softening, too, but the pages went on turning,
    the eyes moved.
In such a miasma of battles, martyrs, and catastrophes,
    if some hard-ass professor
Had asked me to explain effect or cause, I would have said,
    stoically,
"Gnostics buttered bridges," or "Spice wrote Charlemagne."

And after all the years, decades after the flunked exams,
    after the memorized
Periodic table has shrunken to fifty elements in my mind —
    including oxygen, including hydrogen —
The names I was tested for come back, as though the vine
    of centuries had been shaken,
And they had dropped here unrequired: Erasmus, Thomas of
    Aquinas, Lorenzo de Medici.
What names could call back their brief habits of flesh,
    though they woke
The very stars? Awakenings, enlightenments, I have thought
    of as vast cities, unoccupied.
The place of poetry is darker, and the unremitting test
    of love and poetry
Plies its single-minded question: what, if anything, will last?

I have by heart a few lines. I know the life of the mind
    is not the only life,
But Saturday night in the mall, I wish there were a farther
    aisle,
Another range of stores: planks laid with capers and olives,
Hemp stalls where the just-weaned kids bleat for the nannies.
    I can almost smell the prawns.
I can almost hear the sandals clacking on the cobblestones
    and the thick vowels of the auctioneer.
On the lip of the imitation fountain, I sit with the spikeheads
    and the Lutherans,
Studying the dresses and shoes, and the little Fiberglas god —
    like a phrase translated once and forgotten:
"The only principality is Rome; the only language is Latin."

Pure Mathematics

I have been told it is all theory in the end, no letter
    applying to a number
That stands for a thing, no principal accruing interest
    in a practical account,
Only the pure joy of theory and the theory of theories
    I heard
My drunk mathematician friend try to explain one night
    in a Country & Western bar,
Collaring the few who'd listen, truckdrivers and ex-jocks,
    to show them sure proof
That followed some premise they didn't care to understand.

We might have been crabs comprehending opera or sibyls
    poking the blue entrails of frogs,
And still his logic accumulated napkins in an orderly pile
    that the red-haired waitress,
Who finally asked him to leave, swept away and dumped
    under the counter in a barrel.
And driving home later on that icy farm-to-market road,
    he was still
Expounding, jubilantly, maniacally, as the way weaved
    and the universal values
Of arbitrary points unrolled an infinitely expanding line.

It was the clean relish of his mind that made me forget
    the hard curves, the trees
That loomed from the snowy shoulders down to the creek.
    My mind was never like that.
What I liked best the year I studied calculus was chance
    error, my lame prayer

That I might arrive like Columbus, who came by wrong
    to the right unknown. Nothing applied.
O hypothetical mind, we many who are left behind know
    we can never know. We
Stand grounded under the twin wings of the infinite sign.

But in the banking offices near the train station in Rome
    where the currency
Is exchanged — kroners for deutschemarks, yen for lire —
    it all applies.
A button is pushed and the great curve flashes onscreen,
    reckoning all commodities,
All livestock, grains and ores, all modes of production,
    all strikes against management.
And all mismanagement, all mines, ships, wells, and guns
    represent and are represented by
The fluctuation of that curve against the undeviating line

That neither gold, nor oil, nor missiles banked in silos
    will ever turn to theory.
In one of the white lies that numbers tell, I stood there
    while the dollar went
Down on its knees and prayed to the Allah of the Saudis
    and the Buddha of the Japanese
To rise changed into millions of lire, to sing in the grotto
    of the vendor's palm,
O wherever I went all that day, not knowing the language,
    and no difference too
Small, no knowledge that would not be turned to advantage.

Just So

The last time I marveled at any thing of the hands
it was three flawless burnished spheres in a cage,
all carved from a single block of cherry by a man

who built his own house from scraps, warped boards,
bits of siding and odd shingles left over from jobs
he'd contracted earlier when construction was going

all over the valley, affording him trucks and boats,
allowing drugs that led, inevitably, to breakdowns,
and several seemingly irreversible lives in hospitals,

then therapy so expensive the banks took everything
back except for these stony and begrudging acres
set so deep in hills you have to come four-wheel

on a miasma of dirt roads with axle-popping ruts.
You have to move carefully, crossing his icy yard.
The porch is cluttered. The dog looks undecided

whether it is finally fierce, magisterial, or shy.
But you would think it design the way the different
types of siding and the tricolored roof blend with

and complement the colors of the boulders and trees.
The creek beneath the house, when the last leaves
have fallen, makes the exact sound of the leaves,

and the whole place is so sternly quiet and peaceable
the essential feeling it evokes is closer to fear
than to beauty, if fear is more perfect unrealized.

But do not say it was fear that trued his shaky hand
to reliable work, or that too much of character
is ever implied in the self-erasing planing of a board.

Those who believe symphonies underwritten by stigma
have spoken too often and well of their own silence.
And this man, my cousin, aspires to a simpler art.

Now that he's married again and accepted Christ,
you would not guess that first fortune he lost,
or the nights he lay out here, wanting only to die

into the infinite white oaks and Edens of the owls.
And if you did not know it was of a single piece,
you would think the trick of the cage, with its

fleurs-de-lis crawling each bar to the lion at the crest,
was not his patient and steady attention to craft,
but how he maneuvered the reddish spheres inside,

just so they seem almost cardinals, they seem almost
to sing out of their own vanity and longing to fly;
but they are, say it, only what they are, no more

than chunks of wood partially freed from the trunk.
And this rough house is not the pieces of his life,
though the planks are nailed together well enough;

he can live inside as though it were his own mind
he'd made that habitable, and so might be satisfied
awhile and let go unfinished his plan for paradise.

Every Day There Are New Memos

Fact-fluffed, appended with dates, they drift down, O bount-
    iful accountings, O grim disbursements!
I take them from the box. I take them from the groggy hand
    that moved for no more purpose
Than to record the slow minutes of meetings where nothing
    was really resolved,
But I keep thinking that those names hoisted above small towns
    and splashed
With orange paint across the silver tanks of water towers
Mark the final defeat of the block plant and the soybean fields,
    and I keep believing
That those luminous nicknames, Blade and Superstar, as they
    surface in Queens or the South Bronx —
Spraypainted so artfully on the sides of subway cars that one
Has to look two or three times beneath curiosity and admiration
    to make out the lettering —
Represent our surest victories over glass, concrete, and steel.

In a time of vague and courteous doubt, in the quantum amnesia,
    in the fretful face
Of failed loves, I have put my faith in the locally signed work:
    John Payne
Hardware, Red Mullins Rebuilt and Guaranteed Transmissions,
    Bob and Stump Stevenson
Of Stevenson Brothers Furniture. Everywhere else the family
    business is lost. Everywhere else
The anonymous acme of the great purchase rewards and subsumes
    all minor concerns,
Subcontracting for its own name a tone: soporific, indigenous
    to no tongue,
But projecting a gray aura of confidence, of accurate machines.

This is why I work very hard to make out the name Delray Jenks
      under the Prudential sign.
I imagine him sneaking out at night in his old shoes to repossess
      his city with paint,
Writing soliloquies on sidewalks, aphorisms in public restrooms —

But we do not truly read them, the entries are so profligate
      they seem cracks
Ramifying up walls, flawing the marble patina of our days.
Yet in just this dubious way the leopard and the fox express
      their clear boundaries,
The braggart signals to the saint from across the abyss.
Whatever was brought low is lifted high. Whatever was
      nameless shines.
The insides of buses are like phonebooks listing the fierce
      and the promiscuous,
And in the woods, the lovers who carve their initials deep
Into the beeches are like Whitman reviewing his own poetry.
      Proud flesh,
Proud glamour of the self, my joy now is to sign this openly,
      I who often wanted to be no one
And dreaded more than stitches the roll approaching my name.

An Explanation of the Exhibit

That day the Challenger cracked and spread an immolating spider
     across the televised sky,
my daughter, home with chicken pox, sat with me in the den.
All day, together, we must have seen the replay twenty times,
     a dark sport, easy as ball,
though each time we watched, we knew that someone real was
dying beautifully off one white leg that curled toward the sea.

The barely noticeable scar between her eyes shrinks and lightens,
     and the long silences
framed by explanations are repeated hundreds of times a year.
     Each autumn when
we go to see the geese break formation over the familiar marsh,
     she's quieter,
as though their flight were a slow walk across a usual street.

And things here, today, perhaps because they're still, bore her.
This capsule Shepard rode is spud, stump, used grocery bag.
     Even the jeep back from the moon,
silver as an aging actress, is dented in places, more glamorous
     from farther off,
and when the model of our solar system hums and starts to revolve,
she points to the hidden motor, the thin cables that work the spheres.

And maybe she's right not to ask what casts that shadow beyond.
     Space *is* boring,
its nearest stars inhospitable, too far to reach, not just
     in this century, but in the next,
as it drags its ponderous camera outward, recording slopes
     of what appear to be rocks, idling
over far deserts, probing with Einsteinian brain and Ptolemaic heart.

The free arcade is better, toggled and strobed, a screen of meteors,
      through which she weaves
her own green craft like a crocheting needle through a tablecloth,
and I have to nudge her back along the arrows of the exhibit hall.
I think each blip is death's toy; each rocket, misguided prayer.
      That scalpel held
to the autopsy of God is no bow to rub the music of the spheres.

Lunch in the cafeteria, the Muzak is more like the starchy Pepsis
      we drink from paper cups,
the spineless planks of whiting and slaw we dip from plastic tubs.
Outside the window, von Braun's V2 is frail and fishlike.
Australopithecus in the evolutionary line, it almost seems to cringe
      beside Apollo, prone on its side
but hung like some cosmic elephant with 12.5 million pounds of thrust.

In sleep, the weight of my daughter, rearranging itself on my arm,
      is heavier when we walk out again,
and I'm thinking how much she'd want to see the little submarine
and these five smaller missiles that are neat as the flanks of deer.
      Because her eyelids twitch,
I'm thinking of wings, her dreams, and remembering the moon ride
      I'd promised her right before lunch,
I'm wondering if I should shake her gently now and wake her up.

IV. The Weepers

Pastoral for Derrida

When coyotes hunt, they come as a clean silence
comes to a text. They come from beyond myths
out of the tree line along the creek and pick
a lamb, a tender and easy word. Spoken once,
it won't be changed, and the ewe bawls all day.
All night under flocculent covers, we give her up
to sleep. The next morning, clear and warm,
the sun's a word we'd want to mean happiness,
but the ewe holds her place, perfecting rage,
and lets the burs knot her wool, and goes down
wobbly on scuffed hocks, muddy with grief.
The cry swells deep in her hot sheep heart
and floats out to us like pieces of her lamb,
spleen and scruff, follicles pebbly as toads,
so we see, not just lamb, but our own kids
that perishable, that liable to be broken on fangs.
Like any parent, I'd think too much of peril.
My worries blur from the herd of likelihood,
far from the soft, hospitable centers of dens,
where the lawnmower throws a shrapnel of wire,
where the deaf missile strays from the silo.
Still, I wonder who or what she means to call —
not us, certainly, any more than clouds or trees —
or if the petition, repeating, means at all,
or is some hunger that longs beyond capacity
of stomachs, with no object in grain or grass.
It could be any thing or one, sheep or man:
in elms, summer squalls or winter whines;
the cat howls on the barbed, necessary prick.
The times I'd cry all day, I finally was the cry

itself and not myself, but sob on lemony sob
like wave on wave breaking against a rock,
autonomous, purer once there were no tears.
Any cry begins profound, in the ore of words,
in the lungs' pink lode and honeycomb. It
thickens like gravity in the unsuckled udder.
Hear it, and you'd know the theme was loss,
or how every cry's a compass with no needle
that offers, anyway, some vague direction,
as the disbeliever offers up his prayer
to the crazed heavens, to the absent gods.
And surely even the ewe must know
it does no good to cry, to carry this tune
until it carries her — "to the dogs," we'd say,
to butcher and marl. Neither does it help
to ply the tools of facile affection, sweet
words that would succor, hands that would
soothe the hives of demonstrative afflictions,
though these mean well. Poor culpable
spirit, unreckoning Dostoevski among the beasts —
I would stand, too, and send each
bleat like a shovel into the flinty air
under the hermeneutical circle of the vulture.

The Sadness of Early Afternoons

Maybe the Sheikh gets to toss his oil wells in the dice,
But here in the living room it's wan more than warm,
After coffee and sweet rolls, when the vacuum groans
Ahead of her like a troll, and life is longer than she
Thought in high school, and time is the critical dust
That floats above the stereo before the kids return.
She buffs her nails or plucks from her domestic well
A flaccid cup of Metrecal, and irons while the TV unfolds
An evolving plot that is less like a line than a tree,
With each pictured life stretching its fabulous branch:
Blackmail, divorce, passion in caves, prisons, gazebos,
Dead-ending into the pink bud of each commercial. Soaps
Are all like this, playing out the reel of eventualities,
Each unlikely trope securing fate in the continuing
Episode. The girl who scoured sinks and polished crystal
In the Emersons' kitchen had money. She slowly sank in.
She was someone from the past, which will come later.
But when it comes, the answers only pose more questions.
Will the chauffeur be sent back to Poland? What object,
Yet unseen, spread that mortifying shock on Erica's face?
Was it Chad or Josh? — these names that call to the unborn.
And there are séances where poverty speaks to good fortune.
There are so many deep gazes, cryptic sighs, and far away
The new actress muttering into the mystery of the telephone;
So many doctors in trouble for something that is not quite
Clear, some miswielded scalpel or drunken ambiguous procedure . . .
The past is everything, though for now, all that may be seen
Is a soliloquy, the particulars of which will not be fully
Comprehended until next week, when Lance returns from Salvador,
Making Jessica erotically glad, but throwing the whole gilded

Household of the Kenwoods, those sourpuss Episcopalians,
A curve of destitution, and then the scene changes: a blond
Girl we do not know yet is struggling up a seaside hill.
The sense is incomplete, though we can guess why Ashley,
Our helpless and innocent Rapunzel, is pawning the rubies.
And it *is* like life, where the leading cause of infidelity
Is amnesia, with every plot carried out and entered into
The rec room of the veterans' hospital, into the contiguous
Gravy of days that are plotless for the unemployed,
The unemployable, when the last foodstamps have been
Thrown into the ante in the impossible bluff on a straight,
And the ace of obsessions has gone unplayed — except here
On the box. It is not that we do not know what will happen,
But how will it happen? What unforeseeable kink
Will draw the dead back up into the camera's glyptic eye?
And who will tell Gerard, caught in that far set: that
Child, the one you thought was yours, was never yours,
And you yourself are not who you think you are. Already
Tomorrow's table is being set for another guest, some hot
Latin fluff or venerable tabloid star to be written in
As you are written off. And this is what has been held back:
The prognosis, the story beneath that new bandage and lump,
Is like the exegesis you were always too ready to accept,
Not understanding what we . . . if only we, out here, could come
Into the story and tell you . . . that night you were run down
And lay unconscious, the doctor who operated was not drunk,
But bought off by Kirsten, your own wife, who conspired
With your unknown brother, the Sheikh. And that procedure
That would reverse everything, bring you roaring out of
The wheelchair, has been discovered already, but will be

Used against you in the end, perhaps because our desire
Is that you join us here in the suburbs and the projects,
In Peoria and Schenectady. In the vast harem boredom keeps,
We are offering you the sinlessness of our own unlived lives.

In Manufacturing

If one of us, because his wife had left,
Pulled a base tube from the press too late or soon,
And another, because a child had cried
All night, brought her caliper too quickly
Around its flange, a hundred or more tubes
Might come off the line thin-walled, out-of-round.
And if the noise drowned a loud joke to drone,
When you stooped to hear, the saw would kick
A crimped or kinked tube you could never catch
Until it swung toward the next machine.
Like medicine, the line was meant to work
One way. Nothing went better than planned,
Though the plan's one phrase repeated again
And again, while the tubes, soft from furnaces,
Diminished in the dies, a hot and balky work
I would not choose for a daughter or son,
Though part of the dullest business is fun.
And on dog days all our horseplay was ice
That set us running between cooling vats
Where the tubes went tallowy and vanished
And erupted again in cowls of green smoke
While the cranes roared overhead like angels.
And then the boss would lay the gospel down
Because someone complained from far away,
So to this day when I stand in a green pool
Under a clanking air conditioner
Or read how a plane goes mysteriously down
I wonder if it might have been us or some
Other crew who did or did not do what
Now is certain, or if the error is even human.

The Weepers

How could they do it, as though a smoky wind
had blasted their inflamed eyes or they sat
in a shut cupboard dicing a basket of leeks,
when they were not hurt and had hurt no one?
Their tragedies were average. It was not
the age of tears, yet often I saw them start,
kneeling at plain altars or leaning over bars,
their first glove-muffled sobs like the first
tremors of an earthquake that heaves up cities
or those first salty jars that prime the pump,
promulgating the troughs, creeks, and rivers
that fill the famous lakes and oceans of tears.
How they shook then. In hiccuppy assaults.
With the full mortal heart. They wept spasms.
They wept in great, undignified, blubbering fits,
and what could we do to console them?
How would we dry them out or pick them up
who went to pieces, broke down, or burst out,
invoking, in their sniffling, our own names,
our bleak deeds, our most embarrassing dreams?
Did they prefer things streaked and blurred,
the colors of houses merging with the colors
of trees, the lawns melting into the streets,
the dun sky running and smearing the station
where the vague buses were always going away?
Pity was too common for them, and sympathy.
Neither were they truly sad. They wept best
when there was no legitimate reason for tears,
no recent widow walking her mongoloid son,
no deaf student sodomized behind the gym,

no mendicant with his lyrics of a suicidal girl.
They did not believe in despots or atomic bombs.
They wept on celebration days, when picnics
were spread by pretty lakes or bronze plaques
were engraved with their names. They wept
sagas and epics. It was their talent to weep.
Their happiness was as fluent as their grief.
And yet I did not like them. Their seriousness
was exclusive and oppressive. I sat in the back
with the stoics while they moved to the front
in strict allegiance to the superiority of tears.
I could not resist the temptation to test one
with a practical joke, a dirge pitched off-key,
an orange water pistol trained on lamentations,
a Chaucerian fart let against momentousness.
I hated those sycophants who followed them,
porcupines of funeral homes, elderly senators
with patriotic speeches, nostalgic Irish priests —
those whores who knew all the tricks to arouse
the prolonged and mystical coming of tears.
But when I cried, all casket-rattling stopped,
jokes withered, my own life rose like bread,
and no one, not in the whole becalmed world
of measured feeling, was so ripely green, freed
in that compulsive, purblind, repetitious release.

Serious Partying

The little hits of psychopharmaceutical bliss
the street kids still call purple microdots
were delivered in plain Ziploc sandwich bags

and went three hits for seven dollars. One
would bring bees to paper flowers or zing
a sewer line up a face, and on that night,

after each of us ate three like ham-on-rye,
salami, and corned beef from mother's kitchen,
we rode with the dealers in their custom van

out past one of the churches called Mount Zion,
then walked a marshy logging road to a cave
where their commune thrived. We went down

ladders through the snaggled gum of a sinkhole —
boulder on boulder like great gray potatoes,
omphalos of leaves, foil of ruined picnics,

arrows and swastikas blowtorched on walls —
and when the tunnel flared to chamber,
they showed us where Choctaws had slept on skins,

and, in one pool, moved an impossible bolt
of subterranean light, a kind of Xerox of fish
the eyes could copy upward onto shadow. Things

they'd stolen were stacked in alphabetized rows
and marked for passage north: stereo receivers
and speakers still packed in factory boxes,

silver settings in velvet casks and collections
of Rosenthal crystal they'd come across
by accident or purpose on daylight kamikaze

tours of vacationers' homes. All this
was maybe truly dictated by Rimbaud and Marx.
I'm convinced the place was real. Bangled girls

from up east come south to save the rural poor
swayed there in the strobe-lit Texas swing with
guru crooks. They'd wired the place themselves.

My uncle, who thinks America's gone to hell,
might have dreamed this, jolting his John Deere
through the black bottoms, praying for rocks

to fall on communists, pederasts, and humanists.
What I saw might have been silly foreshadowing,
the underground we'd live a tense while with

hell above us, beans charred magically on their vines,
but, clearly, we had fun. Even after I saw
the gun, I laughed and could not stop laughing.

Last Night Among the Very Young

Soon I will go for the last time and sit
All night with the drunks in the loud club
And lift a great stein to the brave dancers
And crawl again through urinary shrubs
And cry hard for the lime mermaid to rise
From the pool, and ride across the city
With the five dudes in the black Camaro.
Once more I will shout at the bicyclists
And go punching mailboxes off their posts.
This time I will be both guide and advice.
Having no wars, no gods, no oppressors,
No brothels, I have learned the easy way,
Rattling the tracks by the closed factory.
First there will be the old people's tower,
Then the cement tortoise of the schoolyard.
The two lights in my suburb are the things
I have almost forgotten, the secrets
That can be learned only at three and five,
When the sky is yellowest and the clacks
Of ball on ball in the after-hours joint
Are like gavels descending in courtrooms.
Nothing will be left but the used body.
Nothing will be left untransformed by neon.
This is the least hour of the last place
And the hand that once wrote the address
Has long vanished, and the address goes up
In a bland curlicue over the ashtray.
Soon there will be no one to tell the lie
Of bullfighting and trolling for marlin,
Of what the fifties were like in Cuba —

Only a bored girl who wipes the tables,
Only her vague shadow through the dark glass.
But you over there! Charmaine! your nylons
The manifestos of revolutions,
Your pink nails the promises Ponce de León
Heard and followed into the sweet mangroves:
Come up from the mirror and take the car,
The house, the garden with its muddy weight.
Though I bend there again this afternoon
And suffer the excruciating light
And find fresh Floridas in the lilies;
Though I love my house, my wife and sons,
This is the clay that hangs on the trowel,
The adolescence after the second childhood.

Life of Sundays

Down the street, someone must be praying, and though I don't
Go there anymore, I want to at times, to hear the diction
And the tone, though the English pronoun for God is obsolete —

What goes on is devotion, which wouldn't change if I heard:
The polished sermon, the upright's arpeggios of vacant notes.
What else could unite widows, bankers, children, and ghosts?

And those faces are so good as they tilt their smiles upward
To the rostrum that represents law, and the minister who
Represents God beams like the white palm of the good hand

Of Christ raised behind the baptistry to signal the multitude,
Which I am not among, though I feel the abundance of calm
And know the beatitude so well I do not have to imagine it,

Or the polite old ones who gather after the service to chat,
Or the ritual linen of Sunday tables that are already set.
More than any other days, Sundays stand in unvarying rows

That beg attention: there is that studied verisimilitude
Of sanctuary, so even mud and bitten weeds look dressed up
For some eye in the distant past, some remote kingdom

Where the pastures are crossed by thoroughly symbolic rivers.
That is why the syntax of prayers is so often reversed,
Aimed toward the dead who clearly have not gone ahead

But returned to prior things, a vista of angels and sheep,
A desert where men in robes and sandals gather by a tree.
Hushed stores, all day that sense a bell is about to ring —

I recognized it, waking up, before I weighed the bulk of news
Or saw Saturday night's cars parked randomly along the curb,
And though I had no prayer, I wanted to offer something

Or ask for something, perhaps out of habit, but as the past
Must always be honored unconsciously, formally, and persists
On this first and singular day, though I think of it as last.